*Paid for by donations*

*from the*

*Mount Laurel Community*

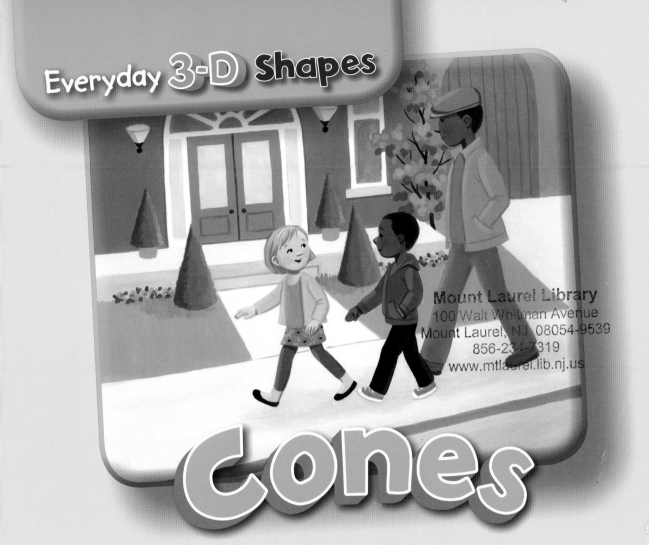

Everyday 3-D Shapes

# Cones

by Laura Hamilton Waxman
illustrated by Kathryn Mitter

Content Consultant: Paula J. Maida, PhD,
Department of Mathematics, Western Connecticut State University

magic wagon

visit us at
**www.abdopublishing.com**

Published by Magic Wagon, a division of the ABDO Group, PO Box 398166,
Minneapolis, MN 55439. Copyright © 2013 by Abdo Consulting Group, Inc.
International copyrights reserved in all countries. All rights reserved. No part of
this book may be reproduced in any form without written permission from the
publisher.

Looking Glass Library™ is a trademark and logo of Magic Wagon.
Printed in the United States of America, North Mankato, Minnesota.
042012
092012

 THIS BOOK CONTAINS AT LEAST 10% RECYCLED MATERIALS.

Text by Laura Hamilton Waxman
Illustrations by Kathryn Mitter
Edited by Rebecca Felix
Series design by Craig Hinton

**Library of Congress Cataloging-in-Publication Data**
Waxman, Laura Hamilton.
Cones / by Laura Hamilton Waxman ; illustrated by Kathryn Mitter.
pages cm -- (Everyday 3-D Shapes)
Content Consultant: Dr. Paula Maida.
ISBN 978-1-61641-872-4
1. Cone--Juvenile literature. 2. Shapes--Juvenile literature. 3. Geometry,
Solid--Juvenile literature. I. Mitter, Kathy, illustrator. II. Title.
QA491.W37 2012
516'.156--dc23
2012007114

Tops are pointy and bottoms round.

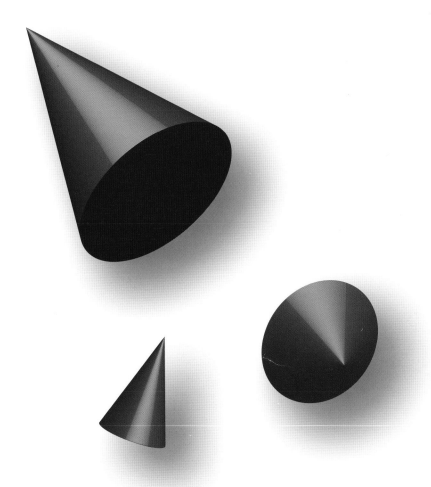

Where can cone shapes be found?

Side views show the pointed top

that spreads out to a wider stop.

Look around for this shape's look.

Search for cones inside this book.

Orange cones keep cars away
as workers fix the street today.

8

Party Lights

10

Jill points out cones glowing bright.

These cones fill the room with light.

Party cones go on your head.

Ben's hat is blue and Jill's is red.

HAPPY BIRTHDAY

13

Cones hold ice cream, cold and sweet.

Ice cream is Ben's favorite treat!

15

Jill gives flowers wrapped up tight.

Ben holds them in a cone of white.

Ben shares his crayons, sharp and new.

A cone-shaped end in every hue.

Tall cloth sides and floor that's sewn.

Sticks hold up this tepee cone!

21

Cones aren't just inside this book.

They're all around you. Take a look!

23

## I Spy a Cone Game

Look around. Find a cone. Then say, "I spy a cone that is . . ." and name its color. Everyone has to guess what cone you see. Then it is someone else's turn to spy a cone. You can guess what it is.

## Count the Cones Game

Choose a room in your home. Count how many cones you can find.

## Glossary

**cone:** a shape with a flat, round bottom and a curving side that meets together at a single point.

**hue:** the color of something.

**round:** something that is circular in shape and has an equal distance from the center to any part of the edge.

**shape:** the form or look something has.